SINGER'S CHOICE

PROFESSIONAL TRACKS FOR SERIOUS SINGERS

SING THE SONGS OF

Jerome Kern

T0078769

2110

Jerome Kern kept very busy during the 1920s. His "Look For The Silver Lining," caught on and in 1925 he began to collaborate regularly with his longtime lyricist Oscar Hammerstein II. In 1927 they wrote the music for Show Boat, a historic show that resulted in such songs as "Make Believe," "Ol' Man River," "Can't Help Lovin' That Man," "Why Do I Love You" and "Bill." It became the most famous of all Jerome Kern musicals.

Kern began to write for Hollywood films in 1929 although he would return to Broadway within a few years. The 1932 film Music In The Air included "The Song Is You" and "I've Told Ev'ry Little Star." Back on Broadway, the 1933 musical Roberta, (which originally starred Bob Hope) introduced "Smoke Gets In Your Eyes" and "Yesterdays." His last Broadway show, 1939's Very Warm For May, included one of Kern's most famous and important compositions, "All The Things You Are." Although Jerome Kern did not care for jazz and hated it when jazz instrumentalists changed the notes of his songs and used them as vehicles for solos, ironically most of his best compositions were perfect for jazz. "All The Things You Are" became one of the most utilized of all chord changes in jazz and the song has been kept alive chiefly due to jazz artists.

Jerome Kern returned to Hollywood in 1935 where he wrote the music for a dozen films. For the 1935 film version of Roberta, starring Fred Astaire and Ginger Rogers, Kern and Hammerstein added some new songs including "I Won't Dance" and "Lovely To Look At." For the Astaire/Rogers follow-up film Swing Time, Kern and Hammerstein wrote "The Way You Look Tonight," "A Fine Romance" and "Pick Yourself Up," a trio of songs all of which immediately became standards. In 1936 Show Boat was given its definitive film version. 1937's High, Wide And Handsome featured Irene Dunne singing the memorable Kern ballad "The Folks Who Live On The Hill," a song later adopted by Peggy Lee. As World War II. began in Europe, in 1940 Kern and Hammerstein wrote the heartfelt "The Last Time I Saw Paris."

For 1942's You Were Never Lovelier, Kern teamed up with lyricist Johnny Mercer for several songs including "I'm Old Fashioned." "Long Ago And Far Away" came from 1944's Cover Girl, a Gene Kelly-Rita Hayworth film.

Active until the end Jerome Kern had just started working on the score of Annie Get Your Gun when he died suddenly in 1945 from a cerebral hemorrhage. He was 60.

-**Scott Yanow,**
author of 11 books including Swing,
Jazz On Film and Jazz On Record 1917-76

SING THE SONGS OF

CONTENTS

©2014 MMO Music Group, Inc. All rights reserved.
ISBN 978-1-941566-05-3

A Fine Romance

Words and Music by
Dorothy Fields and Jerome Kern

A fine ro-mance, with no kiss-es, a fine ro-mance, my
friend, this is; We should be like a cou-ple of hot to-ma-toes,_____ but you're as cold as
yes-ter-day's mashed po-ta-toes._____ A fine ro-mance, you won't nes-tle, a fine
ro-mance, you won't wres-tle; I might as well play bridge with my old maid aunts; I have-n't got a
chance, this is a fine ro-mance._____ A fine ro-mance, my good fel-low, you
take ro-mance, I'll take jel-lo; You're calm-er than the seals in the Arc-tic O-cean;_____
_____ At least they flap their fins to ex-press e-mo-tion._____ A fine ro-mance, with
no quar-rels with no in-sults and all mor-als; I've nev-er mussed the crease in my blue serge

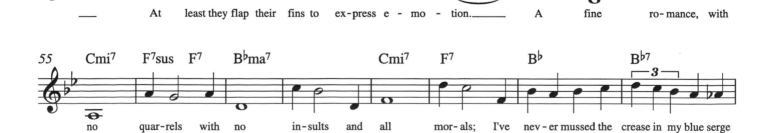

Copyright © 1936 UNIVERSAL - POLYGRAM INTERNATIONAL PUBLISHING, INC. and ALDI MUSIC   Copyright Renewed
This arrangement Copyright © 2014 UNIVERSAL - POLYGRAM INTERNATIONAL PUBLISHING, INC. and ALDI MUSIC
Print Rights for ALDI MUSIC in the U.S. Controlled and Administered by HAPPY ASPEN MUSIC LLC c/o SHAPIRO, BERNSTEIN & CO., INC.
All Rights Reserved   Used by Permission   Reprinted by Permission of Hal Leonard Corporation

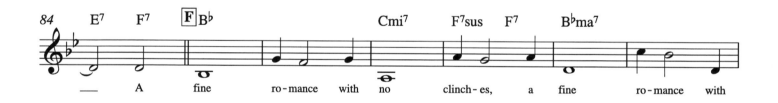

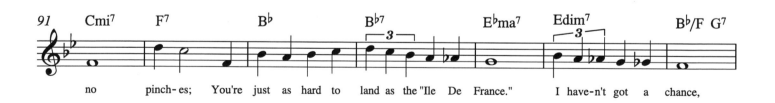

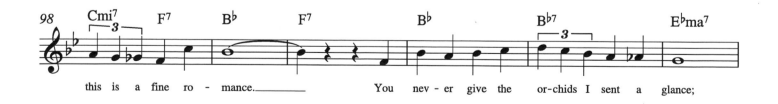

Smoke Gets In Your Eyes

Words and Music by
Otto Harbach and Jerome Kern

Copyright © 1933 UNIVERSAL - POLYGRAM INTERNATIONAL PUBLISHING, INC. Copyright Renewed
This arrangement Copyright © 2014 UNIVERSAL - POLYGRAM INTERNATIONAL PUBLISHING, INC.
All Rights Reserved Used by Permission *Reprinted by Permission of Hal Leonard Corporation*

The Last Time I Saw Paris

Words and Music by
Dorothy Fields and Jerome Kern

A la-dy known as Par-is, ro-man-tic and charm-ing, has left her old com-pan-ions and fad-ed from view; Lone-ly men with lone-ly eyes are seek-ing her in vain; Her streets are where they were but there's no sign of her; She has left the Seine. The last time I saw Par-is, her heart was warm and gay; I heard the laugh-ter of her heart in eve-ry street ca-fé. The last time I saw Par-is the trees were dressed for spring; And lov-ers walked be-neath those trees and birds found songs to sing. I dodged the same old tax-i cabs that I had dodged for years; The cho-rus of their squeak-y horns was mu-sic to my ears. The last time I saw Par-is, her heart was warm and gay; No mat-ter how they change her, I'll re-mem-ber her that way. I'll think of hap-py hours and peo-ple who shared them; Old wo-men sell-ing flow-ers in mar-kets at dawn; Chil-dren who ap-plaud-ed Punch and Ju-dy in the park, and those who danced at night and kept their Par-is bright

Copyright © 1940 UNIVERSAL - POLYGRAM INTERNATIONAL PUBLISHING, INC. Copyright Renewed
This arrangement Copyright © 2014 UNIVERSAL - POLYGRAM INTERNATIONAL PUBLISHING, INC.
All Rights Reserved Used by Permission Reprinted by Permission of Hal Leonard Corporation

till the town went dark._____ The last time I saw Par-is, her heart was warm and gay; I heard the laugh-ter of her heart in eve-ry street ca-fé. The last time I saw Par-is the trees were dressed for spring and lov-ers walked be-neath those trees and birds found songs to sing. I dodged the same old tax-i cabs that I had dodged for years; The cho-rus of their squeak-y horns was mu-sic to my ears. The last time I saw Par-is, her heart was warm and gay; No mat-ter how they change her,___ I'll re-mem-ber her that way.

The Way You Look Tonight

Words and Music by
Dorothy Fields and Jerome Kern

Some day when I'm aw-f'lly low when the world is cold I will feel a glow just think-ing of you and the way you look to - night. Oh, but you're love - ly with your smile so warm and your cheek so soft; There is noth-ing for me but to love you just the way you look to - night.

Copyright © 1936 UNIVERSAL - POLYGRAM INTERNATIONAL PUBLISHING, INC. and ALDI MUSIC   Copyright Renewed
This arrangement Copyright © 2014 UNIVERSAL - POLYGRAM INTERNATIONAL PUBLISHING, INC. and ALDI MUSIC
Print Rights for ALDI MUSIC in the U.S. Controlled and Administered by HAPPY ASPEN MUSIC LLC c/o SHAPIRO, BERNSTEIN & CO., INC.
All Rights Reserved   Used by Permission   *Reprinted by Permission of Hal Leonard Corporation*

Yesterdays

Copyright © 1933 UNIVERSAL - POLYGRAM INTERNATIONAL PUBLISHING, INC. Copyright Renewed
This arrangement Copyright © 2014 UNIVERSAL - POLYGRAM INTERNATIONAL PUBLISHING, INC.
All Rights Reserved   Used by Permission   *Reprinted by Permission of Hal Leonard Corporation*

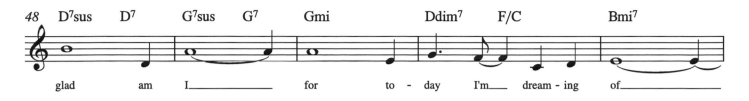

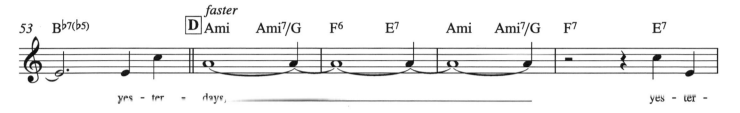

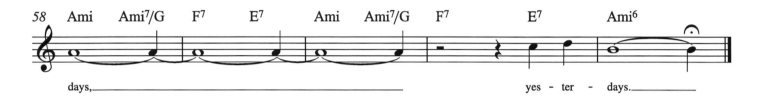

The Folks Who Live On The Hill

Words and Music by
Oscar Hammerstein II and Jerome Kern

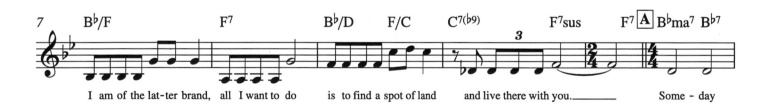

Copyright © 1937 UNIVERSAL - POLYGRAM INTERNATIONAL PUBLISHING, INC.   Copyright Renewed
This arrangement Copyright © 2014 UNIVERSAL - POLYGRAM INTERNATIONAL PUBLISHING, INC.
All Rights Reserved   Used by Permission   *Reprinted by Permission of Hal Leonard Corporation*

Make Believe

Words and Music by
Oscar Hammerstein II and Jerome Kern

Copyright © 1927 UNIVERSAL - POLYGRAM INTERNATIONAL PUBLISHING, INC.   Copyright Renewed
This arrangement Copyright © 2014 UNIVERSAL - POLYGRAM INTERNATIONAL PUBLISHING, INC.
All Rights Reserved   Used by Permission   *Reprinted by Permission of Hal Leonard Corporation*

MMO 2110

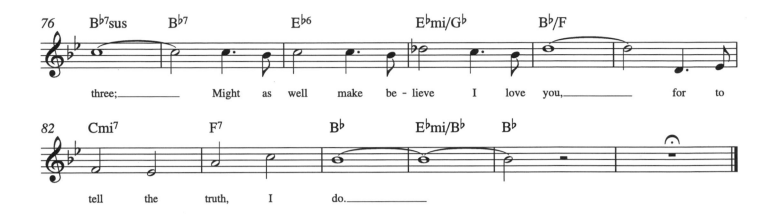

76 — three;_____ Might as well make be - lieve I love you,_____ for to

82 — tell the truth, I do._____

I'm Old Fashioned

Words and Music by
Johnny Mercer and Jerome Kern

I am not such a clev-er one a - bout the lat-est fads; I ad-mit I was nev-er one, a-

5 — dored by lo-cal lads; Not that I ev-er tried to be a saint, I'm the type that they clas-si-fy as

9 — quaint. I'm old fash-ioned, I love the moon-light, I love the old fash-ioned

13 — things; The sound of rain up - on a win-dow pane, the storm-y song that A - pril sings.

18 — This year's fan-cies are pass - ing fan-cies, but sigh-ing sighs, hold-ing hands these my heart un-der-stands.

22 — I'm old fash-ioned, but I don't mind it, that's how I want to be as long as you a - gree to

Copyright © 1942 UNIVERSAL - POLYGRAM INTERNATIONAL PUBLISHING, INC. and THE JOHNNY MERCER FOUNDATION   Copyright Renewed
This arrangement Copyright © 2014 UNIVERSAL - POLYGRAM INTERNATIONAL PUBLISHING, INC. and THE JOHNNY MERCER FOUNDATION
All Rights for THE JOHNNY MERCER FOUNDATION Administered by WB MUSIC CORP.
All Rights Reserved   Used by Permission   *Reprinted by Permission of Hal Leonard Corporation*

stay old fash-ioned with me.   This year's fan-cies are

pass - ing fan-cies, but sigh-ing sighs, hold-ing hands those my heart un - der - stands. I'm old fash-ioned, but

I don't mind it, that's how I want to be as long as you a-gree to stay old fash-ioned with me._____

All The Things You Are

Words and Music by
Oscar Hammerstein II and Jerome Kern

Time and a - gain I've longed for ad-ven - ture; Some-thing to make my heart beat the fast - er;

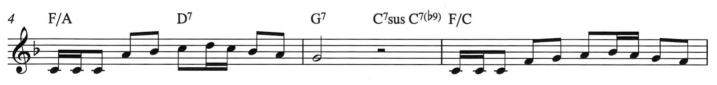

What did I long for? I nev - er real - ly knew. Find-ing your love I found my ad-ven - ture;

Touch-ing your hand, my heart beats the fast - er; All that I want in all of this world is; You are the

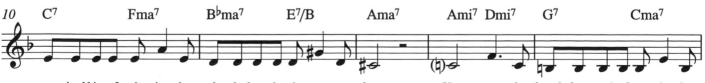

prom-ised kiss of spring time that makes the lone-ly win - ter seem long; You are the breath-less touch of eve-ning that

Copyright © 1939 UNIVERSAL - POLYGRAM INTERNATIONAL PUBLISHING, INC. Copyright Renewed
This arrangement Copyright © 2014 UNIVERSAL - POLYGRAM INTERNATIONAL PUBLISHING, INC.
All Rights Reserved   Used by Permission   *Reprinted by Permission of Hal Leonard Corporation*

16

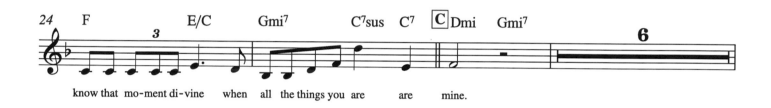

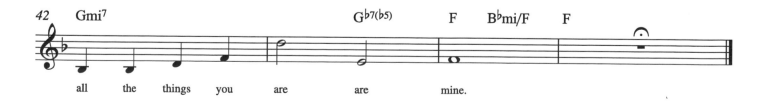

They Didn't Believe Me

Words and Music by
Herbert Reynolds and Jerome Kern

Copyright © 1991 Ramapo Music, Inc. (BMI) International Copyright Secured
All rights reserved   Used by Permission

Other Great Songs from this MMO Series

Vol. 1 - Sing the Songs of George & Ira Gershwin................MMO 2101
Somebody Loves Me • The Man I Love • Bidin' My Time • Someone To Watch Over Me • I've Got A Crush On You • But Not For Me • S'Wonderful • Fascinatin' Rhythm

Vol. 2 - Sing the Songs of Cole Porter............................MMO 2102
Night And Day • You Do Something To Me • Just One Of Those Things • Begin The Beguine • What Is This Thing Called Love • Let's Do It • Love For Sale • I Get A Kick Out Of You

Vol. 3 - Sing the Songs of Irving Berlin ....MMO 2103
Cheek To Cheek • Steppin' Out With My Baby • Let's Face The Music And Dance • Change Partners • Let Yourself Go • Say It Isn't So • Isn't This A Lovely Day • This Year's Kisses • Be Careful, It's My Heart

Vol. 4 - Sing the Songs of Harold Arlen ....MMO 2104
I've Got The World On A String • Down With Love • As Long As I Live • Stormy Weather • I've Got A Right To Sing The Blues • The Blues In The Night • Out Of This World • Come Rain Or Come Shine • My Shining Hour • Hooray For Love

Vol. 5 - Sing More Songs by George & Ira Gershwin, Vol. 2 ....MMO 2105
Of Thee I Sing • Embraceable You • Oh, Lady Be Good • How Long Has This Been Going On? • Summertime • Love Walked In • Nice Work If You Can Get It • I Got Rhythm

Vol. 6 - Sing the Songs of Duke Ellington......................MMO 2106
Do Nothin' Until You Hear From Me • I Got It Bad (And That Ain't Good) • I Let A Song Go Out Of My Heart • It Don't Mean A Thing (If It Ain't Got That Swing) • Mood Indigo • Solitude • Sophisticated Lady • Don't Get Around Much Anymore

Vol. 7 - Sing the Songs of Fats Waller..........................MMO 2107
I'm Gonna Sit Right Down And Write Myself A Letter • I've Got A Feeling I'm Falling • Squeeze Me • S'posin' • Two Sleepy People • Ain't Misbehavin' (I'm Savin' My Love For You) • Honeysuckle Rose • I Can't Give You Anything But Love • It's A Sin To Tell A Lie

Vol. 8 - Sing the Songs of Cole Porter, Vol. 2 ....MMO 2108
You're The Top • Easy To Love • Friendship • Anything Goes • Blow, Gabriel, Blow • You're The Top (Jazz Version) • I Get A Kick Out Of You • Anything Goes (Jazz Version)

Vol. 9 - Sing the Songs of Jimmy McHugh ....MMO 2109
It's A Most Unusual Day • You're a Sweetheart • Don't Blame Me • I Feel A Song Coming On • I'm in the Mood for Love • I Can't Give You Anything But Love • I Can't Believe That You're in Love with Me • On the Sunny Side of the Street • I Must Have That Man

Vol. 10 - Sing the Songs of Jerome Kern ....MMO 2110
A Fine Romance • Smoke Gets In Your Eyes • The Last Time I Saw Paris • The Way You Look Tonight • Yesterdays • The Folks Who Live On The Hill • Make Believe • I'm Old Fashioned • All The Things You Are • They Didn't Believe Me

Vol. 11 - Sing the Songs of Johnny Mercer....................MMO 2111
Come Rain or Come Shine • Charade • The Days of Wine and Roses • Dream • I'm Old Fashioned • I Wanna Be Around • Jeepers Creepers • Moon River • One For My Baby

Vol. 12 - Sing the Songs of Johnny Mercer, Vol. 2............MMO 2112
The Autumn Leaves • Fools Rush In • I Remember You • My Shining Hour • Skylark • Tangerine • Too Marvelous For Words • Mr. Meadowlark

Vol. 13 - Sing the Songs of Rodgers & Hart..................MMO 2113
I Didn't Know What Time It Was • My Funny Valentine • Nobody's Heart Belongs To Me • A Ship Without A Sail • Dancing On The Ceiling • It Never Entered My Mind • There's A Small Hotel • Where Or When

Vol. 14 - Sing the Songs of Harry Warren ....MMO 2114
You'll Never Know • The More I See You • I Wish I Knew • This Is Always • I Had The Craziest Dream • I Only Have Eyes For You • Jeepers Creepers • That's Amore • Serenade In Blue

Music Minus One
50 Executive Boulevard · Elmsford, New York 10523-1325
914-592-1188 · e-mail: info@musicminusone.com
www.musicminusone.com

MMO 2110

ISBN 978-1-941566-05-3